Materials

Glass

Chris Oxlade

Heinemann
LIBRARY

www.heinemann.co.uk/library
Visit our website to find out more information about Heinemann Library books.

To Order:

 Phone 44 (0) 1865 888066

Send a fax to 44 (0) 1865 314091

Visit the Heinemann Library Bookshop at www.heinemann.co.uk/library to browse our catalogue and order online.

First published in Great Britain by Heinemann Library, Halley Court, Jordan Hill, Oxford OX2 8EJ, a division of Reed Educational and Professional Publishing Ltd.
Heinemann is a registered trademark of Reed Educational and Professional Publishing Ltd.

OXFORD MELBOURNE AUCKLAND JOHANNESBURG BLANTYRE
GABORONE IBADAN PORTSMOUTH (NH) USA CHICAGO

Designed by Storeybooks
Originated by Dot Gradations Ltd
Printed by South China Printing in Hong Kong/China

ISBN 0 431 03743 4 (hardback)
06 05 04 03 02
10 9 8 7 6 5 4 3 2 1

ISBN 0 431 03748 5 (paperback)
06 05 04 03 02
10 9 8 7 6 5 4 3 2 1

British Library Cataloguing in Publication Data
Oxlade, Chris
Glass. – (Materials)
1. Glass
I. Title
620.1'44

Acknowledgements

Abode p.9; Barnaby's Picture Library p.16; Bruce Coleman Collection/Pacific Stock p.26; Corbis p.29, /James L Amos p.4, /Lawrence Manning p.24, Phil Schermeister p.15, /H David Seawell p.12, /Vince Streano p.10, /William J Warren p.7, /Nik Wheeler p.8; Crafts Council/JaneMcDonald p.17; Oxford Scientific Films/Colin Monteath p.27; Pilkington p.13; Powerstock Zefa pp.6, 11; PPL Library p.25; Science Photo Library /Victor de Schwanberg p.14, /Pascal Goetgheluck p.19; Trip/S Grant p.18; Tudor Photography pp. 5, 22; View /Dennis Gilbert p.20, /Philip Bier p. 23.

Cover photograph reproduced with permission of Tudor Photography.

Every effort has been made to contact copyright holders of any material reproduced in this book. Any omissions will be rectified in subsequent printings if notice is given to the publishers.

Contents

You can find words shown in bold, **like this**, in the glossary.

What is glass?

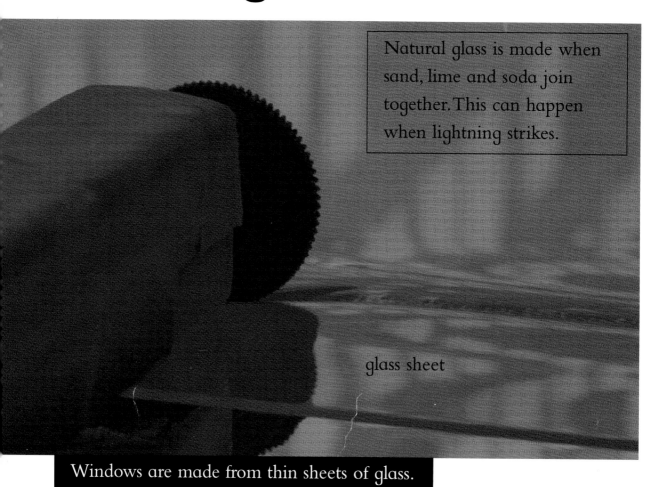

Natural glass is made when sand, lime and soda join together. This can happen when lightning strikes.

glass sheet

Windows are made from thin sheets of glass.

Most glass is made by people in factories.
This thin sheet of glass has just been made.

Glass is waterproof material and you can see through it. We make many different things from glass.

We say a material is **transparent** when we can see through it.

All these things are made from glass.

vase

jug

bowl

drinking glass

Breaking glass

sharp edges

Broken pieces of glass have sharp edges.

Glass objects break into pieces if they are dropped or if they are hit. Because glass breaks like this, we say that it is **brittle**.

Glass is odourless. This means it has no smell.

Glass for doors and windows is made strong to stop it shattering into sharp pieces. This special glass is called safety glass. It may shatter into tiny round pieces, or it may just crack.

cracks

This special glass is called safety glass.

7

See-through glass

Chemicals are added to colour glass.

coloured glass

All glass lets light through. Some glass is **transparent**. You can see straight through transparent glass. Some glass is coloured with **chemicals**. Some glass is clear.

opaque glass

Sometimes opaque glass like this is called 'frosted'. Why do you think this is?

This bathroom window has opaque glass for privacy.

Some glass is **opaque**. It lets light through but you cannot see straight through it. Bathroom windows often have opaque glass so that nobody can see in.

Heat and chemicals

These fire fighters wear protective clothing made from glass fibres.

glass fibre clothing

fire fighter

Glass does not burn when it is heated up. Fire fighters wear fabrics made with thin **fibres** of glass to protect themselves from flames.

Scientists store **chemicals** in glass bottles and tubes. This is because glass is not damaged by most chemicals. Strong chemicals would eat away metal or plastic.

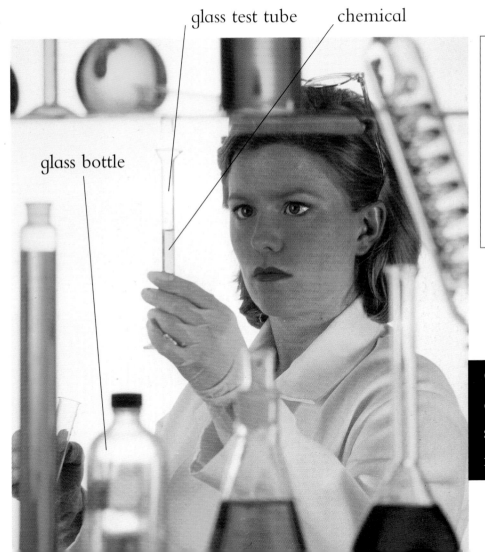

glass test tube

chemical

glass bottle

Although glass is brittle it is one of the strongest substances known.

Chemicals can be stored safely in glass.

Making glass

furnace

molten glass

This worker wears protective clothing near the hot furnace.

Glass is mostly made from sand, just like the sand on a beach. The sand is mixed with other **chemicals**. Then it is heated until it **melts** to make a thick liquid.

When the hot liquid cools down, it sets to make glass. To make thin sheets of glass, the liquid is spread onto the top of a huge pool of very hot, **molten** metal.

This glass has been made into thin sheets.

The hot, runny metal used in this process is molten tin.

— glass sheet

13

Shaping glass

glass bottles

These bottles have been made in moulds.

Some glass objects are made in **moulds**. Hot, liquid glass is poured into a mould. When the glass has cooled, the mould is opened and the object is taken out.

Some objects are made by glass blowing. A glass blower puts a blob of hot, liquid glass on the end of a tube. He blows along the tube and the glass blows up like a balloon, then sets.

A glass blower blows air into the molten glass.

blowpipe

glass blower

Making patterns

A cutting disc is used to make patterns on glass.

You can decorate glass by making patterns on its surface. This artist is making patterns on a glass bottle by cutting into them with a **cutting disc**.

You can also make patterns by **etching**. Patterns are painted onto the glass with **chemicals** that eat away at the surface. A pattern is left when the chemicals are wiped off.

etched pattern

This glass door has a pattern etched into it.

Mirrors and lenses

We can see ourselves and the things behind us in a mirror.

A mirror is made of a sheet of glass. The smooth back surface of the glass is painted with silvery paint. Light that goes into the mirror bounces off the paint and out again.

A magnifying glass has a piece of glass in it called a lens. The lens is thicker in the middle than at the edges. It bends light to make things look bigger than they really are.

Have you ever used a magnifying glass? How did it help you?

A magnifying glass helps you to examine small things closely.

ant

Glass in buildings

Glass used in windows is called glazing.

glazing

Windows let light from the sun into buildings.
They also stop heat escaping from warm buildings
and keep the wind and rain out.

Did you know that the Romans cast glass on
to flat stones to make the first window-panes?

In cold countries, many buildings have double glazing to keep the insides of the buildings warm. Each window has two sheets of glass, with a small gap between the sheets.

As well as keeping a building warmer, double glazing can reduce noise from outside.

Double glazing cuts down heat loss from buildings.

double glazed window

double glazed door

Decorating with glass

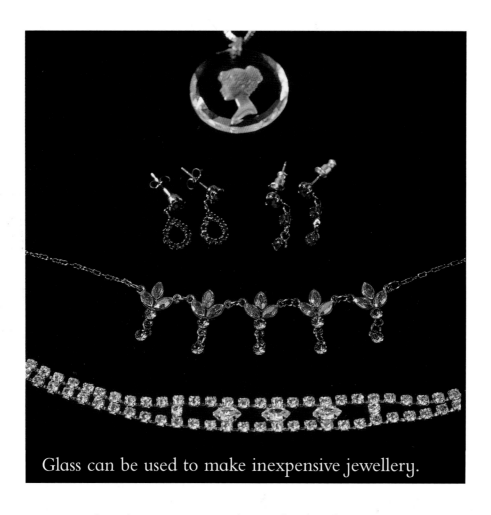

Glass can be used to make inexpensive jewellery.

Glass often looks pretty when light bounces off it, or goes through it. Some **jewellers** use glass instead of expensive gemstones such as diamonds to make jewellery and ornaments.

Small pieces of coloured glass are used to make patterns. These **stained glass** windows look beautiful when sunlight from outside floods through them.

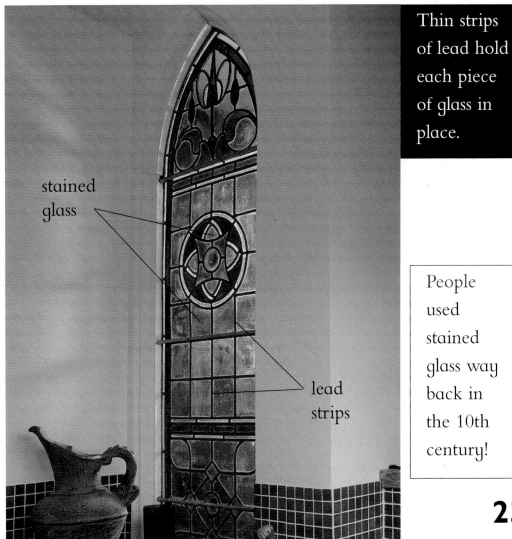

stained glass

lead strips

Thin strips of lead hold each piece of glass in place.

People used stained glass way back in the 10th century!

23

High-tech glass

These glass fibres are called optical fibres.

optical
fibres

plastic
casing

This cable has long, thin glass fibres inside it.
Flashes of light travel along the fibres, carrying
telephone calls.

This boat is being made from a very strong material called glass-reinforced plastic, or GRP. The material is made of glass and plastic. It is a stronger material than glass or plastic on their own.

This boat's hull is made from glass-reinforced plastic.

hull

boat-builder

Recycling glass

Are there recycling bins where you live? Do you recycle used glass? Why do you think recycling is a good idea?

used glass

bin

Recycling glass reduces waste.

Glass bottles, jars and other glass objects can be used again to make new glass things. This is called recycling. Sometimes there are bins for glass of different colours at recycling centres.

The glass is taken to a glass-making **factory**. It is sorted into different colours and smashed into pieces. Then it is **melted** and made into new objects.

This glass has been sorted into different colours.

Fact file

Most glass is made in **factories**. Some glass occurs **naturally**.

Plain glass is **brittle**. It smashes into pieces easily. Safety glass is much stronger than plain glass.

Glass lets light through. It can be plain or coloured.

Glass does not burn. It goes soft and runny when it gets very hot.

Glass is waterproof. It does not rot away when it is wet.

Electricity does not flow through glass.

Heat does flow through glass, but not very well.

Glass is not attracted by **magnets**.

Would you believe it?

Some of the biggest glass objects in the world are mirrors in huge telescopes. Scientists use telescopes to look into space. The biggest telescope mirror is six metres across. That is as wide as three grown-ups lying end to end!

telescope

The mirror in the Hale Telescope at the Mount Palomar Observatory in the USA is used to collect and focus the light from stars and galaxies up to about 2000 million light years away!

Telescopes like this have huge mirrors in them.

29

Glossary

a
b
c
d
e
f
g
h
i
j
k
l
m
n
o
p
q
r
s
t
u
v
w
x
y
z

brittle   snaps or breaks when it is bent, stretched or dropped on a hard surface

chemicals   materials that are used in factories and homes to do many jobs, including cleaning and protecting.

cutting disc   tool for cutting glass. It has a circle of metal with a sharp edge. As the disc spins, the edge cuts into the glass.

electricity   form of energy. We use electricity to make electric machines work.

etching   making a pattern on the surface of a material by letting chemicals eat away at the surface

factory   place where things are made using machines

fibre thin thread of material. Glass fibres are threads of glass as thin as a hair.

jeweller person who makes jewellery

magnet object that pulls iron and steel to it

melt turn from solid to liquid

molten solid material that is heated until it melts

mould block of material that is hollowed out in the shape of an object

natural comes from plants, animals or rocks in the earth

opaque lets light through but is not see-through

stained glass glass that has been coloured by chemicals

transparent see-through

a
b
c
d
e
f
g
h
i
j
k
l
m
n
o
p
q
r
s
t
u
v
w
x
y
z

More books to read

I Can Help Recycle Rubbish by V. Smith, Franklin Watts, 2001

Science All Around Me: Materials by Karen Bryant-Mole, Heinemann Library, 1996

Science Files: Glass by Steve Parker, Heinemann Library, 2001

Shooting Stars: Material Matters by Robert Roland, Belitha Press, 2002

Starting With Science: Solids, Liquids and Gases by Deborah Hodge, Heinemann Library, 1997

Index